For

_____

From

_____

_____

Date _____

Published in Nashville, Tennessee, by Tommy Nelson. Tommy Nelson is a registered trademark of Thomas Nelson, Inc.

MY LITTLE BIBLE
© 1991 by Thomas Nelson, Inc.
Illustrations © 1991 by Stephanie Britt.
Stories retold by Mary Hollingsworth.

MY LITTLE BIBLE PROMISES
Copyright © 1994 by Thomas Nelson, Inc.
Illustrations © 1994 by Stephanie McFetridge Britt.
Compiled by Brenda C. Ward.

MY LITTLE PRAYERS
© 1993 by Thomas Nelson, Inc.
Illustrations © 1993 by Stephanie Britt.
Compiled by Brenda C. Ward.
The publisher has made every effort to locate the owners of all copyrighted material and to obtain permission to reprint the prayers in this book. Any errors are unintentional, and corrections will be made in future editions if necessary. The publishers acknowledge special thanks for the permission received from the following: Celebration for "The Butterfly Song" by Brian Howard, © 1974, 1975 by Celebration. "A Great Gray Elephant" courtesy of the National Society to Prevent Blindness. "Sometimes by Step" by Rich Mullins, © 1992 BMG Songs, Inc./Kid Brothers of St. Frank Publishing.

Scripture quotations are from the *International Children's Bible, New Century Version*, © 1986, 1988, 1999 by Thomas Nelson, Inc. Entries marked KJV are from the King James Version.

MFGR.: Hung Hing / Shenzhen, China / December 2009 / PPO #100188

Illustrated by Stephanie Britt

MY BIG
Little Bible

A Division of Thomas Nelson Publishers

NASHVILLE   DALLAS   MEXICO CITY   RIO DE JANEIRO

Contents

My Little Bible

Old Testament Stories

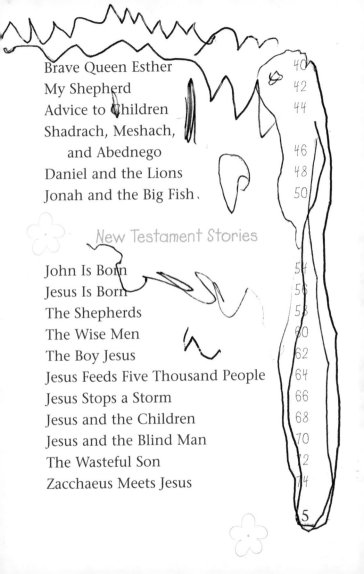

My Little Bible Promises

My Little Prayers

my little Bible

Stories Retold by
Mary Hollingsworth

Illustrations by
Stephanie McFetridge Britt

"May the Lord bless you and keep you. May the Lord show you his kindness. May he have mercy on you. May the Lord watch over you and give you peace."

NUMBERS 6:24–26

OLD
TESTAMENT
STORIES

God Made the World

God made the world. And He made
everything in it. He made the sun and
moon. He made seas and dry land. He
made plants. He made fish, birds, and
animals. Then He made man and
woman.

God was happy with what He had
made.

Genesis 1:1–25

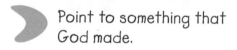

Point to something that
God made.

Adam and Eve

The man and woman God made were named Adam and Eve. They lived in a beautiful garden called Eden. They took care of the garden for God. The garden was full of wonderful fruit trees and plants. God let Adam name all the animals.

Adam and Eve were very happy in Eden.

Genesis 1:26–2:25

 Can you find the lion in the picture?

Noah's Big Boat

People on earth had become bad. Noah was the only good man. God decided to flood the earth with water. So, He told Noah to build a big boat to save his family. God sent two of each animal for Noah to put on the boat.

It rained for forty days and nights. Water covered everything. But everyone on the big boat was safe and dry.

Genesis 6:9–8:22

Where is *Noah* in the picture?

Joseph's Special Coat

❁   ❁   ❁

Jacob had twelve sons, and Joseph was his favorite. Jacob gave Joseph a special coat. Then Joseph's brothers became angry. They sold Joseph to some men going to Egypt.

Joseph became a slave for one of the king's workers. And that's just where God wanted him to be.

Genesis 37, 39:1–6

What colors are in Joseph's coat?

Baby Moses

When Moses was a baby, his mother had to hide him from the mean king of Egypt. She made a baby boat for him. She hid Moses in the boat in the Nile River.

The king's daughter found Moses and adopted him. Moses grew up in the king's own house, just as God had planned.

Exodus 1:22–2:10

 Who found baby Moses in the river?

A Burning Bush

When Moses was older he saw a burning bush. But the bush did not burn up. Moses went toward the bush, and God's voice spoke from the bush. "Moses, do not come closer. Take off your shoes. You are on holy ground."

Then God asked Moses to rescue His people from Egypt.

Exodus 3:1–20

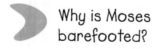

Why is Moses barefooted?

Leaving Egypt

Moses and his brother Aaron went to see the king of Egypt. They said, "God wants you to let His people leave Egypt." The king said, "No." So, God made ten terrible things happen to Egypt.

Finally, the king let God's people go. And Moses led them out of Egypt so they wouldn't be slaves.

Exodus 7:10–12:33, 14:30–31

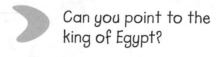

Can you point to the king of Egypt?

God's Ten Laws

After God's people left Egypt, God gave them ten laws. He wanted them to obey these laws. He wrote the laws on big stones and gave the stones to Moses.

These ten laws helped God's people to be pure and holy. The laws are called the Ten Commandments.

Exodus 20:1–17, 24:12–14, 32:15–16

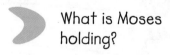

What is Moses holding?

26

Jericho's Walls Fall Down

God wanted the Israelites to capture the city of Jericho. Now, Jericho had big, tall walls around it. So, God had the people march around the city once a day for six days. On the seventh day, He had them go around seven times. Then He had them blow their horns and shout. And the walls of Jericho fell down.

The Israelites captured the city because they obeyed God.

Joshua 6:1–17, 20

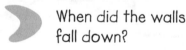

When did the walls fall down?

28

Samson and Delilah

Samson was the strongest man who ever lived. What made him strong was a secret. Delilah was the woman Samson loved. She tricked him, and he told her his long hair was the secret.

Delilah had Samson's hair cut off while he slept. Then Samson was weak, and his enemies captured him.

Judges 16:4–22

 Do you know a secret? Should you tell it?

Ruth and Naomi

❀ ❀ ❀

Ruth married Naomi's son. But the son died. Then Ruth and Naomi moved to a country called Judah. Naomi's cousin Boaz lived there. He had a big wheat field. Boaz let Ruth pick up grain from his field to feed Naomi.

Boaz soon married Ruth. And they had a son named Obed. Naomi took care of Obed.

Ruth 1–4

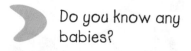

Do you know any babies?

David and the Giant

David was a young, Israelite shepherd. Goliath was a big Philistine soldier. He was nine feet tall! Their countries were enemies.

One day David and Goliath had a fight. Goliath wore armor and had a big spear. David only had his slingshot and five stones. But God helped young David win the battle that day.

1 Samuel 17:4–50

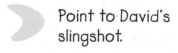 Point to David's slingshot.

34

King David

God chose David to become king. All of God's people met at Hebron. There they made an agreement with David. Then the people poured oil on David's head to make him their king.

David was a great king. He ruled God's people for forty years.

2 Samuel 5:1–12

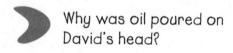

Why was oil poured on David's head?

Solomon Is Wise

When David died, his son Solomon became king. God said, "Solomon, ask for anything you want. I will give it to you." Solomon asked God for wisdom to rule God's people well. God was happy Solomon had asked for wisdom instead of money. So, He made Solomon the wisest and richest man who has ever lived.

1 Kings 3:4–15

Who is the wisest man
God made?

Brave Queen Esther

❀   ❀   ❀

Haman hated God's people, the Jews. He tricked King Xerxes into making a law to kill all the Jews. Esther was the queen, and King Xerxes loved her. But Esther was a Jew. She bravely told the king about Haman's trick. The king became angry and had Haman killed. Brave Esther had saved God's people.

Esther 2–9

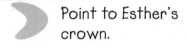
Point to Esther's crown.

My Shepherd

The Lord is like a kind shepherd. And we are like His sheep. He gives us everything we need. He gives us a nice place to sleep, cool water to drink, and good food to eat. He protects us from our enemies. We don't need to be afraid because He is always with us. And we can live with Him forever.

Psalm 23

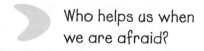
Who helps us when we are afraid?

Advice to Children

Do not forget what your father teaches you. Do what he tells you to do. If you do, you will live a long time. And you will be happy. Keep on loving and trusting your parents. Then God will be happy with you.

Proverbs 3:1–4

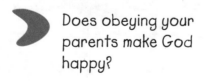

Does obeying your parents make God happy?

Shadrach, Meshach, and Abednego

Shadrach, Meshach, and Abednego loved God. The king of Babylon built an idol for his people to worship. But these men would not worship the idol. So, the king put them in a hot fire. God sent His angel to save them from the fire. The king was amazed and began to worship God, too.

Daniel 3:1–29

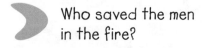 Who saved the men in the fire?

Daniel and the Lions

King Darius made a law for people not to pray to God. But Daniel kept praying to God three times a day. So, the king threw Daniel in a den of lions. God loved Daniel and kept the lions from hurting him. The king was surprised to find Daniel alive. Then King Darius believed in God, too.

Daniel 6:1–23

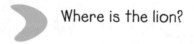

Where is the lion?

Jonah and the Big Fish

God told Jonah to go to Nineveh to preach. But Jonah ran away on a boat. So, God sent a big storm. The men in the boat knew the storm was Jonah's fault. Jonah had not obeyed God. So, they threw Jonah into the sea. Then God sent a big fish to swallow Jonah. After three days, God made the fish spit Jonah onto dry land. Then Jonah went to Nineveh.

Jonah 1–3

How long was Jonah inside the fish?

50

"For God loved the world so much that he gave his only Son. God gave his Son so that whoever believes in him may not be lost, but have eternal life."

JOHN 3:16

NEW
TESTAMENT
STORIES

John Is Born

God's angel told Zechariah that his wife,
Elizabeth, would have a baby. The angel
told Zechariah to name the baby John.
Zechariah didn't believe the angel. So
God wouldn't let him talk until the
baby was born. When the baby came,
the people asked Zechariah to name
him. He wrote, "His name is John."
Then Zechariah could talk again.

Luke 1:5–20, 57–66

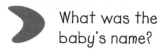

What was the
baby's name?

Jesus Is Born

An angel from God told Mary she would have a baby boy. The baby would be God's only Son. The angel told Mary to name the baby Jesus. He said the baby would grow up to save people from their sins. Later, the baby was born in a stable in Bethlehem. His bed was a box where animals are fed.

Luke 1:26–33, 2:1–7

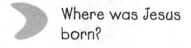

Where was Jesus born?

56

The Shepherds

The night Jesus was born, some shepherds were in the field with their sheep. Suddenly, they saw an angel. And they were afraid. The angel told them not to be afraid. He was bringing good news. He said Jesus the Savior had been born. The shepherds were happy. And they went to worship Jesus.

Luke 2:8–20

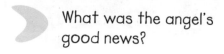

What was the angel's good news?

The Wise Men

Some wise men from the East saw a bright new star. They knew the star was for God's Son. And they wanted to worship Him. So, they followed the star until they found baby Jesus. They gave baby Jesus some very special gifts.

Matthew 2:1–12

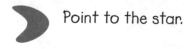

Point to the star.

The Boy Jesus

Jesus went to Jerusalem with His parents. He was twelve years old. After His parents had started home, they couldn't find Jesus. So, they went back to Jerusalem to look for Him. They looked for three days. Finally, they found Him in the temple talking to the teachers about God.

Luke 2:41–52

Where did Jesus' parents find Him?

Jesus Feeds Five Thousand People

More than five thousand people followed Jesus far from town. Jesus taught them and healed the sick. In the afternoon, Jesus's followers wanted to send the people away to find food. But Jesus told them to feed the people themselves. The followers only had five small loaves of bread and two fish.

So, Jesus took the food, thanked God for it, and fed all five thousand people.

Matthew 14:13–21

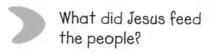

What did Jesus feed the people?

Jesus Stops a Storm

Jesus and His followers were in a boat during a bad storm. Jesus was asleep, and His followers were very scared. They thought Jesus didn't care if they drowned. So, they woke Him up.

Jesus told the storm to be quiet. Then the wind stopped, and the lake became calm. And the followers were amazed at His power!

Mark 4:35–41

Are you ever afraid during a storm?

66

Jesus and the Children

People brought their children to see
Jesus. His followers tried to send the
children away. But Jesus told them to let
the children come to Him. He told his
followers to love God like the little
children do.

Then Jesus took the children in his
arms and blessed them.

Mark 10:13–16

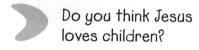
Do you think Jesus
loves children?

Jesus and the Blind Man

❁   ❁   ❁

Bartimaeus was blind. He was sitting beside the road. Then he heard Jesus coming. He called out for Jesus to help him. Jesus said, "Bartimaeus, what do you want me to do?" Bartimaeus said he wanted to see again. Jesus healed Bartimaeus so he could see. Then Bartimaeus followed Jesus.

Mark 10:46–52

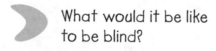

What would it be like
to be blind?

The Wasteful Son

Once the younger of two brothers took his part of their father's money. He went to a faraway country. There he spent all his money. He was poor. He had no food to eat. He took a job feeding pigs. Then he decided to go home. He was sorry for acting so badly.

His father was so happy his son had come home, he gave a party.

Luke 15:11–32

 It is not good to run away from home.

Zacchaeus Meets Jesus

Zacchaeus cheated people by making them pay too much tax. One day Jesus came to town. Zacchaeus was too short to see over the people. So, he climbed into a tree to see Jesus. Jesus saw him and told him to come down. Then Jesus went home with Zacchaeus for dinner. And Zacchaeus never cheated people again.

Luke 19:1–10

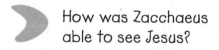

How was Zacchaeus able to see Jesus?

Lazarus Lives Again!

❀ ❀ ❀

Jesus's friend Lazarus died. So, Jesus went to where Lazarus was buried. And Jesus cried. Then Jesus did a wonderful thing! He called out to Lazarus in his grave. He said, "Lazarus, come out!"

Then Lazarus came walking out of the grave. He was alive again! Jesus had raised him from death.

John 11:1–44

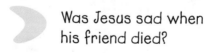

Was Jesus sad when his friend died?

Jesus's Last Supper

The last supper Jesus shared with His followers was called Passover. He held some bread. He said the bread was like His body. Then He held a cup of wine. He said the wine was like His blood. He asked them to remember Him with wine and bread until He comes back.

Luke 22:14–20

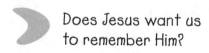

Does Jesus want us to remember Him?

Good News

God's Son, Jesus, was killed on a cross by His enemies. It was a dark, sad day. Jesus's friends took Him down from the cross. They wrapped Him in special cloths and buried Him. But three days later Jesus came back to life!

Jesus is more powerful than death. That is why Jesus can save us from our sins. And that is good news!

John 19:16–20:18

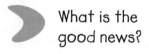

What is the good news?

Jesus Goes
Back to Heaven

Jesus's work on earth was done. He told His followers to tell the whole world the good news about Him. Then Jesus disappeared into a cloud. He went back to heaven.

His followers were still looking into the sky when two men appeared. They told Jesus's followers that Jesus would come back to earth some day.

Acts 1:6–11

Where is Jesus now?

82

Jesus's Followers Share

Jesus's followers shared everything they had. Each person had what he needed to live. The followers gave money, food, and clothes to those who needed it. And God blessed all the followers very much.

Acts 4:32–35

 What can you share?

Saul Meets Jesus

Saul was going to Damascus to hurt Jesus's followers. On the way, a bright light blinded Saul. Then Jesus's voice said, "Saul, I am Jesus. Go to Damascus and wait. Someone will come to tell you what you must do." Three days later, Ananias taught Saul to follow Jesus.

Acts 9:1–19

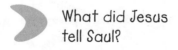

What did Jesus tell Saul?

Peter and the Angel

Peter was in jail. He was sleeping between two soldiers. They had chains on Peter. Soldiers guarded the jail door, too. Suddenly, an angel came. Peter's chains fell off. And the angel led Peter out of the jail. Peter escaped! God saved Peter from his enemies.

Acts 12:6–10

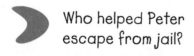

Who helped Peter escape from jail?

Love Other People

The best thing in the world is love.
People who love others are kind and
patient. They are not rude or mean.
They don't brag about themselves.
People who love are not jealous of each
other. They don't get angry easily. And
they are always there when you need
them. They are nice to other people.

1 Corinthians 13

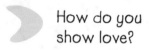

**How do you
show love?**

Obey Your Parents

Children, you should obey your parents the way God wants you to do. This is the right thing to do. God's command says, "Honor your father and your mother." If you do that, God promises you a long, happy life on the earth.

Ephesians 6:1–3

Why should you obey your parents?

Help Others

God wants us to help other people. We should love each other. We should welcome people to our homes. And we should visit people who are in jail. We should show them we care about them.

Hebrews 13:1–3

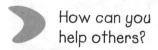

How can you help others?

Jesus Will Come Back!

Someday Jesus will come back from heaven. He said, "I am coming soon!" When He comes, He will bring rewards with Him. He will give gifts to those who do good.

Those who believe in Jesus will go to heaven with Him.

Revelation 22:12–14, 20–21

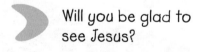

Will you be glad to see Jesus?

"May the Lord bless you and keep you. May the Lord show you his kindness. May he have mercy on you. May the Lord watch over you and give you peace."

NUMBERS 6:24–26

my little
Bible Promises

Compiled by
Brenda C. Ward

Illustrations by
Stephanie McFetridge Britt

I am as happy over your
promises as if I had found
a great treasure.

PSALM 119:162

GOD WILL BE WITH YOU

You can be sure that I will be with you always. I will continue with you until the end of the world.

Matthew 28:20

Come near to God, and
God will come near to you.

James 4:8

You will search for me.
And when you search for me
with all your heart, you will
find me!

Jeremiah 29:13

Being with you will fill me with joy. At your right hand I will find pleasure forever.

Psalm 16:11

I will live with them and
walk with them. And I will be
their God. And they will be
my people.

2 Corinthians 6:16

Those who know the Lord
trust him. He will not leave
those who come to him.

Psalm 9:10

GOD
WILL
GUIDE
YOU

The Lord says, "I will make
you wise. I will show you
where to go. I will guide you
and watch over you."

Psalm 32:8

Lord, you give light to my lamp. The Lord brightens the darkness around me.

2 Samuel 22:29

The Lord himself will go before you. He will be with you. He will not leave you or forget you.

Deuteronomy 31:8

This God is our God forever and ever. He will guide us from now on.

Psalm 48:14

You keep your loving promise. You lead the people you have saved.

Exodus 15:13

But the Spirit gives love, joy, peace, patience, kindness, goodness, faithfulness, gentleness, self-control. . . . We get our new life from the Spirit. So we should follow the Spirit.

Galatians 5:22–25

GOD WILL TAKE CARE OF YOU

Give your worries to the
Lord. He will take care of you.

Psalm 55:22

So our hope is in the Lord. He is our help, our shield to protect us.

Psalm 33:20

You are my hiding place.
You protect me from my
troubles. You fill me with
songs of salvation.

Psalm 32:7

Look at the birds in the air. They don't plant or harvest or store food in barns. But your heavenly Father feeds the birds. And you know that you are worth much more than the birds.

Matthew 6:26

GOD
WILL
BLESS
YOU

Blessed are the pure in heart: for they shall see God.

Matthew 5:8 (KJV)

You give me a better way to
live. So I live as you want
me to.

2 Samuel 22:37

*E*very good action and every
perfect gift is from God.

James 1:17

Blessed are the peacemakers:
for they shall be called the
children of God.

Matthew 5:9 (KJV)

Those who love your
teachings will find true peace.
Nothing will defeat them.

Psalm 119:165

GOD
WILL
FORGIVE
YOU

Yes, if you forgive others for the things they do wrong, then your Father in heaven will also forgive you for the things you do wrong.

Matthew 6:14

Lord, if you punished people for all their sins, no one would be left. But you forgive us. So you are respected.

Psalm 130:3–4

Everyone who believes in Jesus will be forgiven. God will forgive his sins through Jesus.

Acts 10:43

Do not be angry with each other, but forgive each other. If someone does wrong to you, then forgive him. Forgive each other because the Lord forgave you.

Colossians 3:13

We can trust God. He does what is right. He will make us clean from all the wrongs we have done.

1 John 1:9

GOD
WILL
ANSWER
YOU

Continue to ask, and God will give to you. Continue to search, and you will find. Continue to knock, and the door will open for you.

Matthew 7:7

The Lord sees the good
people. He listens to their
prayers.

Psalm 34:15

God listens to us every time we ask him. So we know that he gives us the things that we ask from him.

1 John 5:15

ait for the Lord's help. Be
strong and brave and wait for
the Lord's help.

Psalm 27:14

He will answer the prayers
of the needy. He will not
reject their prayers.

Psalm 102:17

GOD WILL ALWAYS LOVE YOU

Christ's love is greater than any person can ever know. But I pray that you will be able to know that love. Then you can be filled with the fullness of God.

Ephesians 3:19

The Father has loved us so much! He loved us so much that we are called children of God.

1 John 3:1

So these three things
continue forever: faith, hope
and love. And the greatest of
these is love.

1 Corinthians 13:13

Give thanks to the Lord because he is good. His love continues forever.

Psalm 136:1

You are my God, and I will
thank you.
You are my God, and I will
praise your greatness.
Thank the Lord because he
is good.
His love continues forever.

PSALM 118:28–29

my little Prayers

Compiled by
Brenda Ward

Illustrations by
Stephanie McFetridge Britt

The Lord is all I need.
He takes care of me.

PSALM 16:5

MY DAY

Day by day, dear Lord, of Thee
Three things I pray:
To see Thee more clearly,
Love Thee more dearly,
Follow Thee more nearly,
Day by day.

St. Richard of Chichester

Oh God, You are my God,
And I will ever praise You.
I will seek You in the morning,
And I will learn to walk in Your
   ways.
And step by step You'll lead me,
And I will follow You all of my
days.

Rich Mullins

For this new morning with its light,
For rest and shelter of the night,
For health and food,
For love and friends,
For every gift Your goodness sends,
We thank You, gracious Lord. Amen.

Traditional

All for You, dear
 God.
Everything I do,
Or think,
Or say,
The whole day long.
Help me to be good.

Unknown

When the weather is wet,
We must not fret.
When the weather is cold,
We must not scold.
When the weather is warm,
We must not storm...
Be thankful together,
Whatever the weather.

Unknown

He gives food to every living creature.
His love continues forever.

Psalm 136:25

MY
MEALTIME

God is great.
God is good.
Let us thank Him
for our food.

Traditional

Thank you for the world so sweet,
Thank you for the food we eat,
Thank you for the birds that sing,
Thank you, God, for everything!

E. Rutter Leatham

The Lord is good to me,
and so I thank the Lord.
For giving me the things I need:
the sun, the rain, and the
apple seed!
The Lord is good to me.

Traditional

God, we thank you for this food,
For rest and home and all things
   good;
For wind and rain and sun above,
But most of all for those we love.

Maryleona Frost

I go to bed and sleep in peace.
Lord, only you keep me safe.

PSALM 4:8

My Bedtime

Now I lay me down to sleep.
I pray Thee, Lord, my soul to keep.
Your love be with me through
  the night
And wake me with the morning
  light.

Traditional

Lord, keep us safe this night,
Secure from all our fears.
May angels guard us while we sleep,
Till morning light appears.

Traditional

ord, with Your praise we drop off
to sleep.
Carry us through the night,
Make us fresh for the morning.
Hallelujah for the day!
And blessing for the night!

from a Ghanaian fisherman's prayer

Father, we thank You for the night,
And for the pleasant morning light,
For rest and food and loving care,
And all that makes the day so fair.

Help us to do the things we should,
To be to others kind and good;
In all we do and all we say,
To grow more loving every day.

Unknown

Children, obey your parents the way the Lord wants. This is the right thing to do.

EPHESIANS 6:1

MY FAMILY
AND
FRIENDS

God bless all those that I love.
God bless all those that love me.
God bless all those that love
those that I love, and all those
that love those who love me.

New England Sampler

Thank You for my parents, Lord,
and all the fun we've had.
There's no time I love better
than with my mom and dad.

Help me, Lord, to always know
the many ways they care.
For toys and snacks and big bear hugs
and always being there.

When I grow up, I want to be
just like my parents, too.
Because they make me feel so great
and love me just like You.

Beth Burt

May the road rise to meet you,
May the wind be always at your
  back,
May the sun shine warm on your
  face,
The rain fall softly on your fields;
And until we meet again,
May God hold you in the palm of
  His hand.

Traditional, Irish

Dear Lord,

Thank You for my grandparents.

They always have time to read to
me or play games.

They like to tickle and play and
laugh.

And they like ice cream and going
to the park, too.

Mostly though, God, they love me.

Please take care of them, Lord.

I think they must be a lot like You.

Anonymous

Our family's big, our
   house is small;
We're crowded as can be.
But, Father, there's a lot of love
That's shared here happily.

I love my mum and daddy, too;
They keep me safe each day.
But thanks for brothers and sisters,
   Lord;
They have more time to play.

Mary Hollingsworth

228

The Lord is my shepherd.
I have everything I need.

PSALM 23:1

My Favorite Things

Please give me what I ask,
  dear Lord,
If You'd be glad about it.
But if You think it's not for me,
Please help me do without it.

Traditional

Dear Father,
Hear and bless
Thy beasts and singing birds.
And guard with tenderness
Small things that have no
words.

Unknown

A great gray elephant,
A little yellow bee,
A tiny purple violet,
A tall green tree,
A red and white sailboat
On a blue sea—
All these things
You gave to me,
When you made
My eyes to see—
Thank You, God.

*National Society for the
Prevention of Blindness, Inc.*

If I were a butterfly,
I'd thank You, Lord, for giving me
   wings,
And if I were a robin in a tree,
I'd thank You, Lord, that I could
   sing,
And if I were a fish in the sea,
I'd wiggle my tail, and I'd giggle
   with glee,
But I just thank You, Father,
   for making me *me*.

Brian Howard

238

When I am afraid,
I will trust you.

PSALM 56:3

My
Feelings

Dear Lord,
Thank you that I am sometimes
    strong,
    help me when I am still weak;
Thank you that I am sometimes wise,
    help me when I am still foolish;
Thank you that I have sometimes
    done well,
    forgive me the times I have failed
    You;
And teach me to serve You and Your
    world
    with love and faith and truth,
    with hope and grace and good
    humor. Amen

A Swaledale Parish Prayer

I feel happy, Jesus!
I am happy when I laugh with
   friends, or hold a puppy.
I feel happy eating ice cream,
   or listening to a story.
I feel happy when someone says,
   "I love you."
Lord, I am happy because I belong
   to You!
That is the best thing of all to be
   happy about!

Sheryl Crawford

Dear God, my friend is moving,
and I'm so sad.

We've had so much fun together,
and I don't want her to move.

Please help her to find new
friends where she's going so
she won't be lonely.

And help me to make new
friends, too.

Thank You, Jesus, for being my
best friend.

Anonymous

Dear God, be good to me.
The sea is so wide,
and my boat is so small.

The Breton Fisherman's Prayer

Jesus, someone I care for lives
 with You now.
I feel very sad because that person
 is not here.
Sometimes I cry... to let the sadness
 out.
Lord, You say that people who
 live with You are happy.
In heaven, there are angels and
 friends and family.
Jesus, please help me to remember
 that someday we will be together
 again with the ones we love...
And we will live forever with
 You in heaven!

Sheryl Crawford

This is the day that the Lord has made.
Let us rejoice and be glad today!

PSALM 118:24

My Special Days

My Birthday

Dear Lord, I am happy today
  because it is MY BIRTHDAY!
I was born on a day like today.
It was a great day for my family,
  one they could never forget.
Thank You for fun things,
  like cake and candles,
  for family and friends and
  presents and birthday cards.
But most of all, Lord, thank
  You for giving me life!

Sheryl Crawford

254

Christmas

What can I give Him,
Poor as I am?
If I were a shepherd,
I would bring Him a lamb.
If I were a wise man,
I would do my part.
But what can I give Him?
Give Him my heart.

Christina G. Rossetti

Christmas

Away in a manger, no crib for a bed,
The little Lord Jesus laid down
   His sweet head;
The stars in the sky looked
   down where He lay,
The little Lord Jesus, asleep on the hay.
Be near me, Lord Jesus; I ask
   Thee to stay
Close by me for ever, and love me,
   I pray;
Bless all the dear children in
   Thy tender care,
Prepare us for heaven, to live
   with Thee there.

Martin Luther

258

Easter

He is Lord,
He is Lord!
He is risen from the dead
  and He is Lord!
Every knee shall bow;
Every tongue confess,
that Jesus Christ is Lord.

Traditional

The Lord listens when I pray
to him.

PSALM 4:3

My Time with God

Two little eyes to look to God;
Two little ears to hear His word;
Two little feet to walk in His ways;
Two little lips to sing His praise;
Two little hands to do His will;
And one little heart to love Him still.

Traditional

All things bright and
   beautiful,
All creatures great and small,
All things wise and wonderful,
The Lord God made them all.

He gave us eyes to see them,
And lips that we might tell
How great is God Almighty,
Who has made all things well!

Carl Frances Alexander

God be in my head
And in my understanding.
God be in mine eyes
And in my looking.
God be in my mouth
And in my speaking.
God be in my heart
And in my thinking.

Unknown

The Lord's Prayer

Our Father which art in heaven
Hallowed be thy name.
Thy kingdom come.
Thy will be done
   in earth, as it is in heaven.
Give us this day our daily bread.
And forgive us our trespasses,
As we forgive those who trespass
   against us.
And lead us not into temptation,
But deliver us from evil:
For thine is the kingdom,
And the power, and the glory,
For ever. Amen.

Matthew 6:9–13 (KJV)

Stephanie McFetridge Britt is a freelance illustrator for books, greeting cards, and magazines. She has illustrated more than 100 children's books and credits God for the huge success of the *My Little Bible* series. Prior to her freelance work, Britt worked for Hallmark Cards, Inc.